TOOLS FOR CAREGIVERS

- **F&P LEVEL:** A
- **WORD COUNT:** 22

- **CURRICULUM CONNECTIONS:** animals, habitats, nature

Skills to Teach

- **HIGH-FREQUENCY WORDS:** a
- **CONTENT WORDS:** bathes, eats, feeds, flies, hops, lands, robin, sings
- **PUNCTUATION:** exclamation point, periods
- **WORD STUDY:** long e, spelled ea (eats); long e, spelled ee (feeds); long i, spelled ie (flies); short o (robin)
- **TEXT TYPE:** information report

Before Reading Activities

- Read the title and give a simple statement of the main idea.
- Have students "walk" though the book and talk about what they see in the pictures.
- Introduce new vocabulary by having students predict the first letter and locate the word in the text.
- Discuss any unfamiliar concepts that are in the text.

After Reading Activities

This book showcases some common robin actions. Take the class outside. Divide the class into groups. One group is the group of robins that chirps, or sings. This group can only chirp or sing. Another is the robin that hops. This group cannot run or walk. They can only hop. Another flaps its wings (arms) and runs to "fly." They cannot "land" or stop until you say they have spotted a worm! Have the groups rotate and change actions. Which is their favorite? Ask readers what they would like about being a bird. What would they miss about being human?

Tadpole Books are published by Jump!, 5357 Penn Avenue South, Minneapolis, MN 55419, www.jumplibrary.com

Copyright ©2020 Jump!. International copyright reserved in all countries. No part of this book may be reproduced in any form without written permission from the publisher.

Editor: Jenna Trnka **Designer:** Michelle Sonnek

Photo Credits: Mike Truchon/Shutterstock, cover, 14–15; Al Mueller/Adobe Stock, 1; Pascal Huot/Shutterstock, 2bl, 3; dhblac/iStock, 2tr, 4–5; rck_953/Shutterstock, 2mr, 6–7; Tim Zurowski/Shutterstock, 2br, 8–9; JamesBrey/iStock, 2ml, 10–11; BrianEKushner/iStock, 2tl, 12–13; Bonnie Taylor Barry/Shutterstock, 16.

Library of Congress Cataloging-in-Publication Data
Names: Nilsen, Genevieve, author.
Title: Robins / by Genevieve Nilsen.
Description: Tadpole edition. | Minneapolis, MN: Jump!, Inc., (2020) | Series: Backyard animals | Audience: Age 3–6. | Includes index.
Identifiers: LCCN 2019016667 (print) | LCCN 2019018522 (ebook) | ISBN 9781645271109 (ebook) | ISBN 9781645271086 (hardcover: alk. paper) | ISBN 9781645271093 (paperback)
Subjects: LCSH: Robins—Juvenile literature. | American robin—Juvenile literature.
Classification: LCC QL696.P288 (ebook) | LCC QL696.P288 N55 2020 (print) | DDC 598.8/4—dc23
LC record available at https://lccn.loc.gov/2019016667

ANIMALS

ROBINS

by Genevieve Nilsen

TABLE OF CONTENTS

WORDS TO KNOW

bathes

eats

feeds

flies

hops

lands

ROBINS

A robin hops.

worm

A robin eats.

wing

A robin flies.

A robin lands.

chick ▸

A robin feeds.

A robin bathes.

A robin sings!

15

LET'S REVIEW!

Robins have orange feathers on their chest. Can you find the robin in this group of birds?

INDEX